Garth's Wish

Chapter 5
Lesson 76: Murmur Diphthong *AR*
Lexile® Measure: 400L

Printed in the United States of America

Copyright © September 2012 by Reading Horizons

No part of this publication may be reproduced, stored in a retrieval system, or transmitted in any form or by any means, electronic, mechanical, photocopying, recording, or otherwise, without the prior permission of the copyright owner.

ISBN 978-1-62382-034-3

Garth lived with his mother and father in the land of Smarth. Every day, his mother went to the castle to fix fine food for the king's family. His father was a guard at the castle.

Each day, Garth was left alone to clean the barnyard and to take care of the animals. He dreamed of working for King Carl. He wanted to take care of the king's animals.

One night, before his mother and father got home, Garth lay on the grass. He looked up at the sky. He marveled at a huge, shining star. He decided to make a wish.

"Star light, star bright, I want to make a wish tonight," sighed Garth. "I come from a good family. We work hard. I wish I could work for King Carl. I want to take care of his animals."

Garth lay on the grass looking up at the star. Then, he fell asleep. While he was sleeping, a bright light shone down from the star to the Earth. The light was right next to Garth. It lasted for only a moment. In a blink, it was gone.

Garth's mother and father were coming home. They saw the bright light. It startled them. They ran to the light. They saw Garth lying in the grass.

"Wake up, Garth!" cried his mother. "Are you all right? What was that bright light?"

Garth sat up. He rubbed his eyes. He looked around. There, lying on the grass, were some garments. He saw a red, velvet coat with gold trim. He saw white pants and black, shiny boots. The star had granted his wish!

"Oh, Mother, look at these fine clothes!" smiled Garth. "The star has granted my wish! Now I can go with you and Father to the castle. I can work for King Carl!"

Garth and his mother and father worked for King Carl in the castle. They lived happily ever after.

The End

Comprehension Questions

1. This story is about a boy who wished to
   a. be rich.
   b. be a knight.
   c. work for the king.

2. Garth's father was
   a. mean.
   b. a king.
   c. a guard.

3. After the flash of bright light, Garth received some garments. Which one of the following items is NOT a *garment*?
   a. a dress
   b. a computer
   c. a pair of jeans

4. After reading the story, which of the following would you guess is true about Garth?

    a. He likes animals.

    b. He watches a lot of TV.

    c. He has many brothers and sisters.

5. How did Garth know his wish had been granted?

    a. The king called him on the phone.

    b. His mother and father told him that his wish had been granted.

    c. He woke up and saw the clothes that he would wear to work for the king.

Skill Words

barnyard	Garth	marvel	startled
Carl	guard*	Smarth	
garments	hard	star	

Most Common Words

a	food	make	was
after	for	mother	we
all	from	my	went
alone	go	now	were
and	good	of	what
animals	had	one	with
are	has	only	work
around	he	right	worked
at	his	some	working
before	home	take	you
can	I	the	
come	in	them	
could	land	then	
day	last	there	
down	lasted	these	
each	light	they	
earth	lived	to	
every	look	up	
eyes	looked	want	
father	looking	wanted	

Challenge Words

boots	clothes	gone	saw
care	ever	guard*	
castle	family	oh	

*both Skill Word and Challenge Word

15